THE BEST
DAM
BUSINESS BOOK
IN THE WORLD

Volume One - A Fast-Read Introduction to a Twelve-Part Series

WILLIAM E. CASWELL

Published by

 GENERAL STORE
PUBLISHING HOUSE

499 O'Brien Rd., Box 415, Renfrew, Ontario, Canada K7V 4A6
Telephone (613) 432-7697 or 1-800-465-6072
www.gsph.com

ISBN 1-894263-96-0
Printed and bound in Canada

Cover design, formatting and printing by
Custom Printers of Renfrew Ltd.

National Library of Canada Cataloguing in Publication

Caswell, William E., 1939-
   The best dam business book in the world / William E.
Caswell; Jane Karchmar, editor.

Includes bibliographical references and index.
ISBN 1-894263-96-0

   1. Management. I. Karchmar, Jane II. Title.

HF5386.C37 2004   658.4   C2004-902459-0

DEDICATION

To Joel Adams and all those leaders out there
who dream and build a magnificent dam,
following its challenging and very lonely road.

TABLE OF CONTENTS

Preface   i

Acknowledgements   iii

Introduction   v

Chapter 1—Meeting Uncle Len   1

Chapter 2—Why Beavers Fail   5

Chapter 3—Four Very Different Beavers   17

Chapter 4—Starting the Dam   25

Chapter 5—The Secondary Dam   31

Chapter 6—The Food Sanctuary   37

Chapter 7—A Lodge Takes Shape   45

Chapter 8—A Home for Cora and Billy   53

Chapter 9—Alone at Last   59

Epilog   67

Appendix   69

About the Author   81

Notes   83

Index   87

PREFACE

This book is intended for CEOs, to guide them as they pursue their lonely toil to greatness. It is, in fact, a parable of another book, *The Climb to Excellence*, which fills in the blanks of *The Best Dam Business Book in the World*. Each book stands alone, yet together they are intended to make a handsome pair.

Like *The Climb to Excellence*, the work of *The Best Dam Business Book in the World* would not have been possible without the great wealth of business knowledge of those who preceded me.

Studying fifty-five management methodologies, initiated with my colleague, Gene Bellinger of Washington D.C., tossing in my own thirty years of sometimes questionable management, and engaging with one international management consulting enterprise for several years, has led me to the present. Key pillars of published wisdom that should be recognized are the works of Ichak Adizes, including *Corporate Life Cycles* (Prentice Hall, Englewood Cliffs, N.J., 1988). It provides much of the "how to do it right" by letting us understand the natural, unavoidable development of all enterprises. An interesting observation was that the approaches espoused therein could be sustained successfully by breaking many cherished myths about running enterprises.

I hope *The Best Dam Business Book in the World* breaks a few of your myths and confirms what you already know to be just plain common sense.

Bill Caswell

ACKNOWLEDGEMENTS

The careful pursuit of the backbreaking detail of editing, reading, re-reading and offering comments is a job I would like to recognize. It has been persistently, patiently and willing done by three friends to whom I owe a special debt: Peter Beacock of Kitchener, Ontario, Dan Trepanier of Ottawa, Ontario, and Joel Adams of Philadelphia. To you, I give my heartfelt sympathy and thanks. This book would be, to say the least, much less without you. Thanks also to Jane Karchmar, senior editor, General Store Publishing House.

INTRODUCTION

Once upon a time in the great northlands lived a young playful beaver named Billy. Billy the beaver loved nothing more than to plunge from his family's beaver lodge into the cool, clear water, to tumble, to swim, and to go as far as his tail would propel him. His parents warned Billy that he was too aggressive, too impatient, too daring, and that his jumping into water without thinking would get him into trouble. But the youthfully brash Billy didn't care; he was too busy having fun.

On this day, however, something unusual happened. Billy rocketed, unthinkingly, out of his lodge into the cool, pristine water, gobbling a water lily on his way, picking up speed, diving up and down, accelerating until he swam smack-dab right into another beaver. But this wasn't just any beaver! What large, beautiful eyes, what sparkling teeth, what shiny fur, what a curvy shape and what a fabulous tail! For the first time in his young life, Billy's perpetual movement was arrested—put completely on hold. What strange feelings overcame him! The two beavers stared at one another for a few moments and then, unsure of what to do, darted off in opposite directions.

Billy returned to his lodge to explain his strange experience to his dad.

"Ah, Billy," said Dad, "I've been meaning to have this conversation with you about the bats and the buds. It's a story about life that you should know."

So armed, Billy was determined to find this new apparition first thing the next day. He didn't have far to go before he spotted a fabulous undulating body in the early morning misty waters ahead. *What shape, what motor motion of thrust and turning by her tail and the push of her churning webbed feet!* he mused. She had been waiting at exactly the same spot where they had met yesterday. *Such a coincidence*, thought Billy.

Well, readers, as you might suspect, Cora—the name of Billy's new friend—discovered a lot about Billy. In fact, they learned a lot about each other; and in doing so, Billy and Cora became inseparable. They got along famously, diving deep into the lake, cavorting along the nearby riverbank. Cora was not shy about slapping the water surface with her tail, exciting Billy at every thunderous clap. My, they were having fun.

Billy's dad and mom were pleased.

"Billy," advised Dad, "it's now time for you and Cora to set up your own lodge."

Suddenly, Billy understood the gravity of the situation. Building a home was no small matter for a beaver. It meant a new lodge, a new lake, and the construction of a dam. Billy, ever ambitious, told his dad that his lodge and his dam would be the best dam in the beaver world.

"Cora must have the finest possible."

"In that case, Son, you are probably out of my league," opined Dad. "However, Uncle Len is the best dam builder in beaver land. I will ensure he is here to guide you and Cora."

> *"Beaver can stay underwater for at least fifteen minutes. . . . During the winter, when it is out of its lodge, the beaver uses the air bubbles and air spaces found under the ice. The lungs are capable of performing a seventy-five-per-cent exchange of air (compared to the fifteen-per-cent performance rate in humans). A shut-off valve in the cardio-vascular system cuts off the flow of blood to the submerged beaver's extremities, thus allowing an increased blood flow to the brain."* **James Cameron (1)**

CHAPTER ONE
MEETING UNCLE LEN

Uncle Len first met Billy to determine what kind of beaver Billy was. He was dreaming of the greatest dam in the world, but could Billy handle it? Len, the wisest and most experienced beaver in the land, judged Billy's ambitious plans, while beyond most beavers, to still be within the realm of possibility—but of immense difficulty. He found Billy's confidence and eagerness refreshing and he knew that Billy's impatience, daring, and aggressiveness would be assets in the great task before him. Then, with his careful assessing eyes, he looked at Cora. Len could not help but notice her striking teeth. However, more relevant now, was that Cora too was intelligent and ambitious, and she was very supportive of Billy's dreams. She, indeed, was special.

Len was happy to take Billy and Cora under his paw. "We will get on with the business of building the best dam in the world. For it is the dam that determines the size of the lake, the amount of the food supply, and the magnitude of the lodge."

"Cora and I plan to have many kits, so we want a large lodge—all the more reason for building a great dam," enthused Billy.

"Billy, how would you go about building the dam?" asked Uncle Len.

"Well," blurted Billy knowingly, for he was the proud possessor of a master of beaver assembly (mba): "I would find the biggest stream in a new field somewhere, make sure there are lots of poplar trees nearby for food and building materials, and . . ."

"Nice dreams, Billy. But what if there is no such big stream and no large trees within reach of us and within reach of all the beavers that will help us? Perhaps you will need to work with what's available."

"Uncle Len, you're making me think. Now I have to tell you. Over the past few weeks I have been looking at the dams in the area to get some ideas, and frankly, they do not look very dam good. So I thought I must do better than these other beavers. With what you have just said, I have to admit I am wondering if getting this business 'right' is possible. Or is having a great dam just a dream? Am I to resign myself to all the difficulties I see in those other dams?"

"Well said, Billy," offered Len, stroking his grey, furry chin. "My first words to you and Cora are that having a great dam *is* possible. But it is not just luck. There is a proven process that works and has been in place for generations before us. A tour of the forest beyond ours will show us some great dams. However, the dam-building process I am going to share with you does not allow shortcuts. It requires an appreciation and an understanding of what constitutes a great dam, and the discipline to see it through. Yet, it has the flexibility for you to adapt the process to your situation. However, if you are not prepared to expend the energy to learn and then to build accordingly—if you want a quick result or if you are building a great dam just to show off—then this will not be a good partnership. You must be in it for the long haul and for the right reasons. There is no easy answer; it is hard work; but it is smart work. And it is totally doable. Now, if you're still committed to the project, let's go ahead and let's be smart about it."

"Cora and I want the best dam in our world, one that will excite us and excite our children all of our lives."

"We definitely want to go ahead with it," said Cora.

"[Beavers] are very bright and clean. They even take their time crossing the road. They stop, listen, look left and right before making a move." **Ernie Michelburgh (2)**

4

CHAPTER TWO
WHY BEAVERS FAIL

On Uncle Len's advice, our protagonists decided to tour some of the other dams in the forest beyond and use those dams as examples of what to do and what not to do. Swimming their way through ponds, brooks, streams, and rivers, they arrived at a beaver pond called Poplar Grove, coming across a 100-foot-wide dam. After meeting the head beaver, Arthur, they were shown his group's achievements of dam size and the grandeur of the pond, which was huge. Its ten-acre size, average for a beaver pond, was nonetheless impressive. Both Cora and Billy were in awe.

Uncle Len, however, felt otherwise. "Cora," he asked, "why do you want a great dam?"

"Knowing you, this is a serious question," she said, "and I'd better think a bit before I reply." After a few moments she offered the thought: "I want a great dam to fulfill my mission in life—to get profitable results, to have fun while I'm getting results, and for others around me to have fun as we get those results."

Billy then added: "For us, results mean a lake well stocked with food, clean water to drink, a reliable lodge to protect and in which to raise a family. And to profit from all the hard work, so that our later life will be a bit easier."

"Yes," added Cora, "and I think that when all is said and done, you and I should be able to feel very proud of our accomplishments and good about ourselves. Now, let's look for profitable results here."

Cora noticed immediately that the water was not very clear. Looking at the end of the dam, she noted that the flow was not brisk at the overflow sluice, indicating a low churn rate of water. There were obviously some problems there. However, no one seemed concerned. It was Billy who observed that the lodge was small and cramped. Uncle Len remarked that looking for a snack in the pond was a challenge; food was not as plentiful as back home. As well, it was obvious that Arthur was a very busy beaver. Despite the age of his dam, he had no time to himself. When Cora slapped her tail on the water, which normally draws attention, she became aware of a general indifference in this beaver community to it—to things new, she supposed. The beavers were not having fun, and several senior beavers seemed to show signs of not communicating with one another.

"Conclusion, Billy?" Uncle Len turned his statement into a question. "While the dam, at first glance, is impressive, a little deeper look, beyond appearances, shows that the results are not there. Why would that be?" asked the elder beaver, piercingly.

"I'm not sure," Cora began her response, "but I think they must have a lot of problems in this community—more than we can see from our surface viewpoint."

"Remember that point," suggested Uncle Len. "We'll put all this information together at the end of our tours. For the moment, the first lesson is that you cannot get results if you have not resolved the problems under the surface of the organization. No matter what great initiative you plan, the problems will drag you back and not allow you to complete the objectives of your new program. Beavers will become skeptical of, and resigned to, the failure of new initiatives. Who are you serving?" asked Uncle Len.

"Well, as I've already told you," repeated Billy, "our customer is this family—me, Cora, and some future kits. If our parents need a place, they will be our clients, too."

"It's easy to please yourselves as clients. But to attract other satisfied clients, are there other issues to consider?"

Cora, ever the astute student, chirped: "We know that we must have others profit from our dam so that a full complement of the ecosystem will be fulfilled. That is, we have to build with the sales thought that we will attract woodpeckers, swallows, hooded mergansers, black ducks, great blue herons, otters, deer, and moose to our pond."

The following day, Cora, Billy, and Uncle Len swam miles up the river and trudged over great lengths of dry land, tree stumps, and swamp to arrive at another dam site. Called the Swamp Dam, it was even more impressive than the last. It stretched for over two hundred feet across and was five feet high at the center.

"Let's look for results first," suggested Billy. Again it was apparent to our heroes that results were lacking, despite first impressions. "Well this is where my mba comes in," offered Billy. "The fundamental mud-work around the dam is poor; water is seeping out uncontrollably; and although they have clear water, there is not enough of it. The level is a foot below the dam.

"Even I know that a large foundation is needed for the lodge, but look at how puny this one is. And look at the results. What a strange lodge. They have had to prop it up with sticks on the outside because some fundamentals were ignored."

"Well, you picked up on lesson number two very readily," said Uncle Len in a congratulatory tone. "The basics must be in place, first. There are many myths out there about the business of dam building that get passed from generation to generation and are perpetuated by well-meaning advisors. Do not follow them unquestioningly. Be certain that you understand the rationale before you accept supposed wisdoms—even mine. Challenge me at any point. It must make perfect sense to you. If I ever say, 'do it because I said so,' then you will have much to fear from that particular piece of advice.

"There is one more dam that merits your attention; it is yet farther away, so we must rest a day before we go there. But you will be glad you struggled through this trip," said Uncle Len.

True to the prediction, Billy, Cora, and Uncle Len found themselves, two days later, in front of a huge dam. It was 600 feet wide, nine feet high at the centre. Below the main dam was a secondary dam 200 feet wide and six feet high. Behind the dams was a huge lake. Called the Great Northern Dam, any beaver had to be awestruck with its massive image. The lodge was well built, too, and not lacking, as our protagonists searched for signs of real results at the Northern Dam site.

"These beavers have been very effective; they have built what they wanted. Now let's look under the surface," led Billy.

Cora concluded: "From a results perspective, I can see clear water, a good food supply, a strong lodge; I'm impressed."

Billy chimed in, spurred on by Cora's lead: "Beavers from other families are visiting here, so this group appears to be respected enough by its peers to attract them. Even more, look at the deer drinking at the far end, and the great blue herons. The builders of the Great Northern Dam satisfied these prospects and, by their building techniques, sold the advantages of this watering hole to them. What do you see, Uncle Len?"

"I agree with your observations, but I've been watching the interaction of the beavers at the south end of the lake. There are signs of problems. The first point is that they seem to be following one another without question. The one or two beavers that make waves are being drummed out of the group. Secondly, their food supply is enormous; they're spending too much time on food. Something else must be suffering. I don't see any new dam-building techniques; they seem to be resting on the laurels of the past. Wouldn't you agree that even our own dam has more innovation than this one?"

"Yes, but who can question their accomplishments?"

"I concur with you about their degree of achievement; but that should not make us blind to problems. Notice that the amount of new construction is limited, and the tidying up of the site is not happening on a regular basis."

"Yes, I see; it is a bit of a mess compared with home," suggested Cora. "I sense that bureaucracy has gained the upper hand."

"Do you," continued Uncle Len, "think these beavers are having fun? Doesn't the climate seem a bit stifling?"

"Yes, you can see the poor mood; but doesn't that happen to all larger enterprises?"

"My point," countered Uncle Len, "is that it should not be so. That poor result conflicts with one of your goals of success—having fun—stated a few days ago."

"Who is that elder beaver over there?" asked Billy. "Do you know him?"

"No," replied Uncle Len, "but I know of him. He is Edgar, a respected expert on dam process re-engineering, obviously brought in to institute some changes."

"That means some beavers see a need for change," offered Cora positively.

"Maybe yes, maybe no," suggested Uncle Len. "I suspect, although I can't be sure, that the enterprise simply wants to apply a known and proven technique as an ongoing search for improvement."

"Sounds like a good move to me," thought Cora aloud. "In and of itself, it should be a good step. But I would offer that the effort is doomed to failure despite the wisdom of Edgar."

"Herein lies my third point," surmised Uncle Len. "You cannot entertain new initiatives until the enterprise is ready. If you do it too early, it will fail, and as a result reinforce the skepticism that is rampant already in Northern Dam, if I'm any judge."

With these things to think about, the three beavers began the long trek home, avoiding the wolverine trails nearby and the wolf packs howling in the not-too-far distance. They kept to the water as much as possible, taking time to survey the land carefully before they had to emerge from water to cross it. They looked for signs of quietness that the predators seem to elicit from the smaller creatures of the swamp.

"If I am to be of assistance to you both, I'd like to get your interpretation of the three basic conditions required for an enterprise's success," said Uncle Len.

As they scurried along, Cora began: "I think the first lesson was that—"

Suddenly they stopped. Despite their weakened vision out of water, their keen sense of hearing, combined with an overwhelming intense odor, had them pause. Then out of the darkness, claws first, bounded a wolverine, hitting Billy, who was in its line of sight. Billy struggled with all his might to pull himself away from the steely grasp. Billy had no intention of giving up. Almost immediately, Uncle Len sunk his incisors into the wolverine's shank, while simultaneously, Cora whomped its face with her generous, muscular tail. The wolverine yelped and released its claws slightly, allowing Billy a split second to roll away and then slip into the adjacent stream. Cora and Uncle Len, lifting their dragging tails off the ground to gain momentum, were in the stream moments later.

Billy put them at ease: "I'm okay; I have some cuts, but they're not serious." He paused and then continued. "I'm glad we were not alone and could cooperate."

"There's no doubt," said Cora, "that by working together we were able to survive. Alone, none of us would have stood a chance with that nasty wolverine."

Uncle Len smiled to himself. Guiding these young, alert beavers would be an absolute delight. "I think we should continue our travels after some rest," he said. "Let's detour slightly to a beaver lodge not far from here where I know we will be welcomed by an ever-curious friend."

"Amen," said Cora.

"Amen, for sure," echoed Billy.

Arriving at the lodge of Peter Beaver, they found a warm welcome awaiting them. After settling down somewhat from their ordeal, they moved to the third level of the lodge to nibble fresh poplar and alder leaves and to chat. Peter B. was, as expected, infinitely curious about their experiences. Learning of the adventure to absorb three basic lessons, he rubbed his balding head as he quizzed the young ones in order to have them share their findings with him.

Cora began, "Well, Peter B., as I was saying before I was so rudely interrupted by Mr. Nasty in the forest, I think the first lesson is that every beaver group has a backlog of problems that they need to address. I believe that they have to view that as their first priority."

"That's an unusual approach," offered Peter B. "How do you know if you have problems? How do you know what priority to put them in? How do you know how to solve them? How . . ."

"Whoa, whoa," interjected Uncle Len. "Our young entrepreneurs will have answers to those later. However, the one point I want you all to consider is that you can expect about ten problems per beaver in the colony."

"You're kidding? Even in mine?" enquired Peter B.

"Yes, even in yours," affirmed Uncle Len. "Serious, unattended problems beneath the surface."

"Aha," offered Billy. "If you give that kind of leeway we'll hear every little whine and complaint from beavers that should just get on with it and quit complaining."

"Well then, you'd be missing an opportunity, Billy. For, where there is smoke there is fire. Many problems are not obviously important; some are. But whatever we do, we must not trivialize beavers' concerns or we will rue the day."

"As I recall from our discussions," assessed Cora, "if you ignore these problems, then you handicap your enterprise in its ability to move forward."

"That's right, Cora; the enterprise hasn't a chance—full of sound and fury signifying nothing. In other words, you can't win the swimming race with a broken tail. First you need to address the problems of the tail and fix it, and then you have a chance of being a swimming champion. Without fixing the tail, you can never develop full steam; you're left as an also-ran. As for Peter B's skepticism," addressing Peter B. directly, "you only have to try problem discovery one time with your team. Once you see the problems before you, you will no longer doubt that the issues are significant. You will realize that they must be dealt with. Even if you somehow don't agree with the need to move ahead, your support beavers will see the liberating benefits and almost immediately demand that the problems be addressed."

"I don't wish to be disrespectful, Uncle Len, but I'm afraid this sounds very impractical," concluded Billy. "Who has time to sit around contemplating problems when there is serious dam building to be done?"

"The humans say that the woodsman who sharpens his axe cuts far more trees than the one who will not take time to do that. 'Sharpening the axe' is taking the long-term view, while 'cutting trees' is the short-term view. The key is to have balance between both the short term and the long term." Speaking softly to Billy, Len added: "But, Billy, I know you want me to cut to the chase—with real facts. As a leader in problem solving, I make sure the problem-solving exercises take no more than 2% of the beavers' time, while 98% remains for dam building. Secondly, my work at numerous beaver colonies over many years has shown a statistical average of 20:1 return on time invested in problem solving to benefits of that problem solving, within the year."

"I'm beginning to see the light," concluded Billy. "This ties directly into lesson number three. In order to get the results that we all seek— proficiency and its rewards—we apply fine tuning that leads to individual accountability that ties into the total organization's objectives; but only when the colony is ready, not before its time, only after it has wrestled the major problems to the ground successfully. Otherwise we end up in an artificial world where appearances are great, but nobody is happy—and disaster lurks just around the corner—as in the Great Northern Dam."

"Shouldn't lesson number two come in there somewhere?" questioned Peter B.

"I don't know how it fits," said Billy.

"Nor do I," joined in Cora.

"Well, Uncle Len," demanded Peter B., weakly disguising his own curiosity, "what light can you shed on this for these interested young beavers?"

"What is lesson two?" Uncle Len enquired, pausing to await the response.

"It's that you have to learn the management fundamentals," parroted Billy.

"Sounds like a huge bore to me," suggested Cora.

"Rest easy, because you're right," droned Uncle Len. "What could be more mesmerizing than a bunch of management lessons? What we do is reduce the boredom by using lesson number one, problem solving, to tell us which management skills need attention. We address only those. Now there is a sense of necessity and a willingness to learn."

"Ah, yes," offered Peter B. "Before Uncle Len, our beaver colony had no idea how to run meetings painlessly, to keep them precisely to one hour, and to have beavers comment later how much they enjoyed the meetings."

"Sounds like fantasy to me," snorted Billy.

"It's not! Most of the beavers here enjoy meetings! Anyway, you'll see soon enough," admitted Peter B. "It's another one of Uncle Len's liberations. But Len, you'll have to come back here soon and introduce my team to the problem-solving process."

"It'll be a pleasure," confirmed Uncle Len. "Before we leave this point," he continued, "probably the most important of these fundamentals, and the one least understood, is how to manage beavers. Put that one high on your action list."

"As far as I'm concerned," opined Cora, "we learned more than three lessons; I think we developed another lesson from that wolverine: The sum of the efforts of a group exceeds that of the individualized efforts of each beaver—by a long shot. Cooperation is a multiplier."

"You did indeed learn," agreed Uncle Len.

"Perhaps we could take a corollary from the wolverine," offered Billy. "Out of adversity come opportunities. In this case, the adversity of the wolverine taught us a lesson—the benefits of cooperation."

"You've got it, friends," concluded Uncle Len. "Several different pieces of knowledge. However, the three major lessons are basic to all group endeavors. There is no point in expecting success unless you take these three to heart, because without them success won't happen—unless you're lucky and only count the short term when luck is leaning your way. The three lessons (or conversely, the three reasons beaver enterprises fail) are:

1. Find and resolve the backlog of problems first.
2. Discover the missing management skills from the problems above and address them, as needed.
3. Do not begin a new management initiative until most of the problems have been addressed. If you put the cart before the horse, the resulting continuous, inevitable failures will turn your enterprise into a colony of skeptics, not to mention beavers with a lack of self-esteem because of the repeated inability of your group to reach the expected goals. Then begin to make each beaver personally accountable for the individual's part of the whole."

"I see an overriding principle in these three," suggested Cora. "May I say what I think it is?"

"Of course," the others chimed in unison.

"Beavers make great dams, yet beavers are an obstacle to making great dams. So we need to focus on the behavior of beavers—not on technology, not on lectures, not on anything else."

"I hadn't thought of it that way," admitted Uncle Len. "But you're quite right, Cora. Congratulations. Every single technical problem in dam construction that I have helped to resolve has resulted from a beaver behavioral issue. As always," Uncle Len concluded, "I find that the teacher can learn from the student."

> *"A prospector in the area near Flin Flon, Manitoba, watched a beaver moving a large tree upstream against a very fast current. At times it was slipping backwards. Apparently the beaver called for help. In moments, four or five other beaver appeared and moved the tree quite easily into quieter water above the fast current."* **James Cameron (3)**

CHAPTER THREE
FOUR VERY DIFFERENT BEAVERS

With a sense of where they wanted to go, Billy and Cora set out to search for a locale for their dam project. In the space of two days, they inspected several meandering streams through the forest, both near and far, finding they had to reject most sites as inadequate or not appropriate, such as those lacking enough trees nearby; those having a flow too small to create the sort of dam they envisaged; or those already being claimed by other beavers.

Finally, they settled on one. It was a wandering stream, running through a meadow, bordered by a forest some one hundred feet distant on either side. About five hundred feet from their anticipated dam site, the stream ran into a bay, which dumped into a majestic river. Billy and Cora's new family would benefit from both the stream and the river. However the young couple was a little unsure about their choice, as the stream was not robust and the stands of trees were fairly distant.

"Cora, you stay here and guard this site while I get Uncle Len for his opinion on our choice—unless you prefer that I guard the site and you fetch Uncle Len."

"No—staying here is the easier of the tasks. You fetch Uncle Len; I'll keep guard," she volunteered.

To avoid predators, especially coyotes or bears, which were common in this area, Cora remained in the water of the stream, swimming its length, or crawling where it was too shallow, down to the river. Noting the water's clarity and abundant vegetation, she became convinced that they had found an ideal spot. The river with its clear, running water would be a valued extra. She passed back and forth several times to explore the nuances of the dam site, the stream, its mouth at the river, and the river itself.

She took some time for herself. Using the two combing claws of her back feet, she reached underneath the outer guard hairs into her very dense, shorter warming hairs to waterproof herself with oil from her glands. She then groomed her outside longer guard hairs that would keep her body dry, even while in the water. Her teeth were getting a bit long, so she ground them back and forth for wear, finishing off by cutting some saplings for dinner. She settled into a finishing diet of roots, sedges, ferns, and water plants. Cora was content.

Returning a day later, Billy and Uncle Len found Cora had passed an uneventful, but relaxing, night.

"Uncle Len, if this location were perfect," began Billy, "we wouldn't need you here to guide us. But look at the forest stands on either side: they are quite far away and will require us to drag the trees and branches long distances. I suppose I should face the facts and reject this one, because those trees really are quite far away."

Cora, now having adopted the spot as her own, chimed in: "Perhaps that's an important factor, Billy, but the stream and river combination are nearly perfect."

"You will have to make your own choice," suggested Uncle Len. "But let me offer you a guideline that might help; I call it the 80% rule—and it is a rule easily abused. So, listen to me carefully.

"In any new endeavor be content with locating 80% of your objectives and assume you will be able to fill in the remaining 20% later. In this case, if you try to locate a 100% perfect site, you will spend many weeks trying to find it, even if you are able to find it at all. The 80% rule allows you to get on with things, to avoid dither and delays. It is based on having the confidence that, by hook or crook, you will be able to adjust to the missing 20%. And even if you don't adapt to it, you will have 80% of what you want. Think of the alternatives of the choice at the moment: 80% of your wants met if you accept it or 0% if you don't; 80%, while not perfect, is infinitely better than 0%. And if the situation has a time constraint you can easily end up with a choice between almost all that you want or absolutely nothing if the time runs out.

"The danger of the rule is misusing it to excuse doing a good job. In any familiar job, you must seek 100% accuracy, otherwise you will end up with sloppiness on sloppiness. The difference between the two is that the 80% rule applies to a speculative task, while 100% rule applies to a known task. As in most things I hope to share with you, there are no absolutes—the key is to maintain a balance between the two options."

Cora was first to comment: "Well, the 80% rule suits me now because I really want this site. But I'm not sure I understand the difference between the two situations you describe, between applying the 80% or 100% rules."

"I guess that means neither of us understands," offered Billy, "because I certainly don't see the differences either. But I understand the 80% rule for the situation now. I would vote for this site."

"Me too," echoed Cora.

Busily the three beavers began to each gnaw at small nearby trees and drag the token trees to the site to mark it as their own.

Upon returning to the main lodge of Billy's family, they discussed the task before them. Uncle Len explained how he would rally his other known beaver colonies to assist in the project, suggesting Cora do what she could with her own family, too.

Billy had expected that Uncle Len would lead the project, but Uncle Len deferred to the young beavers, indicating that it was "their" project. He would delegate it to them; he would be there, but only as a helper and as a guide.

"I think I want to do it a different way, Uncle Len," began Billy. "Cora and I will be joint leaders of the project. I respect Cora's wisdom, her knowledge, and her equality in this relationship."

Cora was flattered and appreciative: "We can be a dynamic duo!"

"You may be a dynamic duo in the endeavors of your lives," suggested Uncle Len, "but you'll be a miserable failure if you take that approach in carrying on a task, especially a complex task. You will end up creating confusion, splitting the camp in two, and resenting one another. Every task must have a single, final authority and there should be no doubt in any beaver's mind as to who that authority is. Think back on joint leadership projects you have been involved in, even small ones. I imagine that you will recall confusion, delays and disasters.

"While a wise authority will confer with and listen to those offering advice, information or guidance, the authority must make the final decision and be accountable to all for that decision."

"I propose that Billy be that final authority," offered Cora. "I say that because I not only have confidence in Billy, but also because I have confidence in myself. I don't need to have my ego stroked."

After some discussion, in which Billy expressed his admiration for Cora and the strength of her character, and admitted to his own shortcomings and reservations, the two of them concluded that Billy would be the project leader—the sole authority. Uncle Len admired their way of coming to that decision; it would serve them well in their joint life ahead.

Deciding on the details of the dam, the lead planners, Billy, Cora, and Uncle Len began the formation of the executive team to oversee the operation. They added Peter B. to their executive group for his innovative ability and visioning. He was tough to pin down or control, but ideas just flowed out of him. Marc was among their first considerations too, because of his aggressiveness and let's-get-it-done-now attitude. Marc was direct, yet cooperative and open to suggestions. Muddy, next on the list, brought her fine skills for details and precision to the team; she could unerringly calculate the amount of mud, branches, twigs, and trunks required at any point. Carol had a calming disposition and a caring attitude towards all beavers; her empathy for the situations of others put her on everyone's favorite beaver list.

Cora observed: "I think we have a diverse, excellent management team. In fact, it's amazing how different some of these members are." She continued, "While Billy and Marc are direct and to the point, they are a bit careless with details. However, Muddy and Carol seem strong on detail but are less direct in dealing with situations compared to Marc and Billy. In terms of looking ahead, Peter B. has a vision that is only matched by Billy's ability to dream and make those dreams come true. I think I fit here, too. As for empathy with beavers, Carol and I seem to excel at that, while Billy and Marc, I must admit, are often intolerant of others."

"Especially if they're lazy," confirmed Billy.

Uncle Len offered: "It is important to recognize these different animal characteristics and to blend them in all that we do. The four broad categories of animal personality styles, examples of beavers we all know, and their behaviors are as follows:

Producer: George Bushy Tail **P**roductive, busy, impatient, direct
Analyzer: Albert E. Owl **A**nalytical, detailed, precise
Visionary: Billy Gatehead Beaver **V**isionary, has ideas, creative
Friend: Oprah W. Otter **F**riendly, cooperative, soothing

"**P, A, V** and **F.**

"I ask you to notice two significant points:

"One: Some of the above animals have two of the four characteristics; some have just one. No animal has strength in all four characteristics.

"Two: The characteristics are in direct conflict with each other. For example:

> *Producers* (George Bushy Tail) are impatient and always in a hurry. *Friends* (Oprah W. Otter) are patient and reliably slow.

> *Analyzers* (Albert E. Owl) plan carefully and in detail. *Visionaries* (Billy Gatehead) are sometimes chaotic and quick to change their minds; they drive Albert E. Owl crazy.

> *Friends* (Oprah W. Otter) are good with people. *Producers* (George Bushy Tail) are often intolerant of people.

> *Visionaries* (Billy Gatehead) look ahead to the grand picture and the future. *Producers* (George Bushy Tail) want results today and have little concern for what they consider the 'unreal' future.

"That is, the *friends* will always be concerned about other beavers, while it will always be difficult for the *producers* to understand the tolerance and concern that the *friends* have for the 'lazy' ones. In each of the four personality styles, it will be difficult to understand why the opposites to your own style behave the way they do.

"But each of the four brings something indispensable to the table. We need all four to make balanced decisions. Otherwise the decision will be skewed in the 'negative' characteristic lacking the balance. For example, if the *friends* are not present, the *producer's* intolerance for people will skew the resulting decisions away from 'people' considerations. This is true in every case. So we need a balance of 'P, A, V and F' in all decision making."

Cora laughed: "Billy, I love you dearly, but now I think I understand your positive and negative aspects better with PAVF. You are full of drive, 'P', sometimes step on other people's toes, always in a hurry, don't suffer fools gladly and are quite dominant sometimes. Your 'A' is terrible—you lack organization and attention to detail. You don't want to analyze things deeply, but prefer to just plunge into the job and trust that your energy will somehow get it done right. With your ability to dream about a great dam, you clearly have 'V,' that leads all the rest of us forward enthusiastically. You come across pretty hard most of the time, but I now see that that it is an act, perhaps driven by your strong 'P,' but your innate generosity, and the fact that you're soft as fluff when it comes to firing beavers from the job tells me your 'F' is very strong, too."

"Dan McCowan, a naturalist, once watched the activities of two beaver near Banff, Alberta. They were swimming, one following the other, with the rear one frequently touching the leader's tail with its nose. The first beaver led the other to shore, where they both began eating. When McCowan walked towards them waving his arms, the lead beaver quickly disappeared into the water but the second beaver kept right on eating. It was blind." **Fred Bodsworth (4)**

Chapter Four
Starting The Dam

With the core team in place, the dam building began as Billy took on the leadership role, which was quite natural for him because of the combination of his *producing* and *visionary* characteristics. Big trees were felled by a multitude of beavers. Marc was especially *productive,* aggressively cutting trees without consulting anyone else. He was prolific to say the least, but many of his trees fell against other trees, their upper branches preventing them from falling where they could be cut up for the dam.

"Marc," barked Billy, "get Muddy over there with you to plan and *analyze* the details of your cuts so we can benefit from your hard work!"

Muddy, recognizing her usual demand to clean up the chaos of others, scurried over to assist Marc, whether he felt he needed it or not. Now that his trees began to fall more precisely, he recognized the need for Muddy's inputs. She summoned Charlene Beaver, another *analyzer,* leaving her with Marc, so that Muddy could freely move on to her other tasks.

Once the trees were felled, the branches were cut off, with the smaller twigs saved for construction, and the leaves (especially poplar) saved for feeding the many workers. The trunks were cut to a size for ease of dam construction. Moving the large trunks was attempted by six to ten beaver together, but they seemed to be working against one another until Cora arrived to bring *friendly* cooperation to bear, counting out a "one, two, three *heave!"* Then the logs slid effortlessly over the long distance of the ground, one heave at a time, to the dam site.

Peter B. with his *visionary* wont could quickly identify stands of trees that should be addressed first, making the overall job easier. He complained of the inefficiencies and lost opportunities of those around him, voicing his issues to Billy, who had to wrestle with Peter's disturbing concerns. However, *friendly* Carol, recognizing the need to smooth the ruffled fur of impatient Billy and the excited Peter B., stepped between them to referee a compromise for the issues at hand. Peter's information was *analyzed* and detailed by Carol to be put to use for everyone's benefit. Billy calmed down somewhat, and could return his focus to overseeing the grand project.

The dam began to take shape. At the dam site itself, Muddy made sure that the mud packing and twig insertion conformed to her pre-dam *analysis* and calculations. The water was rerouted around one end to avoid impeding the construction, so the job could progress more quickly.

Commented Marc, "I see how we are constructing faster than I might have thought and I have to give credit to Billy. He respects all the workers, allowing them to behave their own way, not judging the behavior, but blending the needs together as he did with Muddy and me."

Cora, more in love than ever with Billy, added: "Yes, he allows each beaver the freedom to do the task its own way. He respects each beaver's individuality and uniqueness."

"I have to say," agreed Muddy, "that he seems willing to take the risk to trust that new beavers will do okay. It's admirable; I wouldn't be able to trust them."

Uncle Len, within earshot of this conversation, added. "Intuitively, Billy understands that each beaver has a different trust gap—the degree to which they will trust someone else to do something. It's especially noticeable of this management team as they apply their 'trust' to those under their charge. But more to the point is that Billy grasps the differences and adjusts the situation to them."

"As I said," continued Muddy, "I don't think I could trust like that. What is his secret?"

"By respecting every beaver's uniqueness and by ensuring a respectful atmosphere over the whole project," explained Uncle Len, "Billy is making the environment conducive to trust."

Brian, a senior seasoned and highly respected dam builder added: "Overcoming the trust gap is only possible within a respectful climate. And cooperation is only possible if the basics of respect and trust are in place. That is why this project is progressing so well. I have been on many jobs where respect and trust were lacking, with predictable, disastrous results. Billy's doing a fine job."

Suddenly there was a loud cry from up front. A huge tree had fallen, trapping Kathy underneath.

"Albert," roared Billy above the din, "that is the second time I have had to draw your attention to the task. You will have to leave the project. Please return to your colony, *now.*"

Billy, although focused on results, knew that safety was being compromised. As considerate as he may have seemed towards the workers, he was not a pushover in a serious situation. He knew the difference between, and could readily balance, the interests of the entire project with the individual interests of the workers.

Remarked Uncle Len quietly to Cora: "Billy, as a single authority, can make those choices and decisions on the spur of the moment." It was said as if to validate and reassure Cora that her decision to allow a single authority was sound.

After three days, the dam was indeed looking like a fine structure. Muddy was taking particular care with the base details. As she swam underneath the water to inspect the work of the others, she admired their dexterity underwater as they applied their hand-like front paws to the twig, rock, and aquatic vegetation insertions and mud-packing routines. Other beavers dove in with appropriately sized branches in their mouths, protected by a flap of skin in the mid-mouth that prevented water from entering their throats. She understood the importance of laying the proper groundwork for the base, to resist the temptation to take shortcuts for the quick satisfaction of others who were impatient for a finished dam. A final mud coating all around sealed and reinforced the structure.

The dam was now three hundred feet long and six feet high at its center. A large lake was forming behind it. A sluice allowed the stream below the dam to flow at the same rate as if the beavers had never appeared. The absence of stagnant water meant that mosquitoes could not lay eggs and while the beavers felt no threat from mosquitoes, they did feel the threat from the humans that lived nearby who would probably not tolerate a beaver pond if it bred mosquitoes.

Billy took stock of the situation. Uncle Len looked on critically but positively. The leader conferred with his group of managers. Len sat in as an advisor. As both a *visionary* looking ahead and a *producer* beaver wanting to move forward quickly, Billy proposed that they now consider the construction of the lodge.

However, respecting the difference of the opinions of others, he was neither surprised nor shocked when Carol suggested they slow down a bit. "I think we should take the time to build a three-foot-high secondary dam in front of the first; the *analysis* of this detail will reduce the main dam pressure by half."

Peter, the *visionary*, opined: "It will give longevity to the entire dam, lodge and food supply."

"My workers," offered Marc, "are tired from having to *produce* so much, but I know I can drive them harder."

"You won't have to, Marc," suggested Cora, "because through my *friendly* persuasion, I have a group ready for a new assignment from Peter B.'s colony."

"Then I'm ready and anxious to push forward with them," stated Marc.

"With all of those inputs, you as a group are making a balanced decision," confirmed Uncle Len. "It is also beneficial because you are resisting the temptation to profit quickly now in favor of profiting more later, despite the pressure of your stakeholders—your family back home wanting a quicker return. In fact, if you did not approach things this way, you could jeopardize Billy's and Cora's future, especially if the dam collapsed due to too much pressure during a heavy rainstorm or any other unexpected event."

While Billy's own tendency was to push ahead and do things himself, he was beginning to realize the advantages of the group personality mix, especially in allowing the *analyzer* thinking that he himself lacked participate for more balanced decision making. He could see that he benefited in the end from allowing the 'A' aspects in—from having *all* the PAVF present.

> "[T]hey became so domesticated as to answer to their name, and follow those to whom they were accustomed . . . and they were as much pleased at being fondled, as any animal I ever saw . . . I was obliged to take them into my house [and] they . . . made not the least dirt, though they were kept in my own sitting-room, where they were the constant companions of the Indian women and children, and were so fond of their company, that when the Indians were absent for any considerable time, the beaver discovered great signs of uneasiness, and on their return shewed equal marks of pleasure by fondling on them, crawling into the laps [and] laying on their backs . . . [They] were remarkably fond of rice and plum-pudding [and ate] partridges and fresh venison." **Samuel Hearne (5)**

> "[Scrapper had the run of the house but he] was in trouble a few times for tearing the wallpaper behind the toilet, and for sharpening his teeth on the water pipe there . . . When spanked or scolded he took the chastising with his head on his hands, emitted a big sigh, sulked a bit, then seemed to forget it . . . Lloyd had been away . . . for ten days. When he came in Scrapper . . . went right to him, nuzzled his face, neck and hair, then nibbled his arm from his right hand up above the elbow. He would take hold of the skin . . . lifting it up about an inch, without pinching or hurting at all. Scrapper [had a] naturally happy disposition [and] was comical and lovable. Often he would climb up on the bed, but only if we were there, sit and groom . . . and roll over to play." **Helen and Lloyd Cook (6)**

CHAPTER FIVE
THE SECONDARY DAM

The management team decided to take a moment to review progress so far by conducting a post-mortem on the construction work to see what they could learn for any future dam building, and especially for the smaller project before them, the secondary dam. With the main dam in place, they instructed half the beavers to return home, offering profuse thanks for their work as well as fresh poplar boughs to carry with them if they wished.

As the team evaluated what they had accomplished and noted improvements they might effect next time around, they came to the situation in which Marc and some other beavers had cut several useless trees, leaving them leaning against other trees. Not only was their tree felling a waste of time and effort—and a danger later, if a high wind should topple them onto an unsuspecting beaver—they also deprived the community of valuable leaf food that would never be reached.

"Marc, you and the other impatient *producer* beavers never look before you leap! You just jump in without thinking; you cause us a lot of anxiety," chirped Muddy. She detested wastage and inefficiency.

Marc offered a perfunctory answer: "Get lost, Muddy. You're no sweetheart as far as I'm concerned. If we waited for the whole world to be lined up to fit the detailed *analysis* of the way you like it, we would never get anything done around here."

"Come on, you two," interrupted Cora, "we have a lot to do and we'll get nowhere if you don't cooperate and learn to respect each other."

"Well," continued Muddy, am I right or am I wrong? Did he cut useless trees or did he not?"

Sensing an opportunity to assist, Uncle Len jumped in. "Supposing that you are 100% right, Muddy, what—"

"She's *not* 100% right!" interjected Marc.

"Marc, in this community of respect, you are not allowed to interrupt me," warned Uncle Len.

Billy added to the notification: "Marc, you'll have your turn. Wait till Uncle Len has finished speaking."

Uncle Len pursued his thought: "Supposing that you are 100% right, Muddy, what do you expect to accomplish by pointing the finger at Marc?"

"I bloody well want to get him to think of all the grief he's causing us," she remonstrated. "Maybe he'll smarten up."

Patiently, Uncle Len continued: "Marc, having heard Muddy's well-chosen words, are you ready to change your ways?"

"What I'm ready to do is bite Muddy on her fat beaver tail."

"Muddy," questioned Uncle Len, "if Marc bites you on the tail, does that get us closer to a solution?"

"He's not going to get away with talking to me like that. He's—"

Cora rushed in, in an attempt to save the situation. "Quiet, everyone! I think I know where Uncle Len is going with this. He's trying to show that pointing the finger doesn't get us any closer to a solution."

"Well said, Cora," congratulated Uncle Len, "But it's worse than that. Pointing the finger, even at an 'obvious' person, moves us further and further away from a solution."

"I imagine, Uncle Len, you're about to give us another rule," said Billy supportively.

"Yes, two rules, actually. The first one I call the *perversity of blame* rule:

> "If you seek a solution, do not attempt to blame anyone for the situation. In fact draw the culpable person into the solution process. Conversely, the moment you blame, you set the scene for *not* arriving at a solution. So, if you like solutions, stop blaming. It has the reverse reaction to that intended; it will always prevent a solution. Humans blame and they go to war because of blame. We don't want to be like humans."

There was quiet all around. Billy broke the silence. "Marc, how do you think we can avoid cutting trees that won't fall properly?" as he took up Uncle Len's challenge to involve Marc in the solution.

"I think we already have the answer," suggested Marc. "Pair up a super cutter like me with a super detailer like Muddy. It's like a pilot and a navigator. It combines busyness with precision."

No one could argue with Marc's logic. Muddy spoke sheepishly. "Marc, I'm sorry I got carried away. Uncle Len is right."

"You know," concluded Marc, "he is. For my part, I'll try not to be so defensive."

Cora enquired: "Uncle Len, you said *two* rules. What is the second rule? Is it related to the first?"

"No," replied Uncle Len. "It's not related to the first; it just happened at the same time as the first in that interaction between Marc and Muddy. Less a rule than a truism, it is that *conflict is unavoidable*. No matter how 'good' we try to be, we cannot avoid conflict. We cannot avoid it because the four styles of *producer, analyzer, visionary,* and *friend* won't let us avoid it. The four styles are in conflict with each other as we stated before. Since we need all four styles to get a balanced decision, we inherit the four conflicts that must accompany the good decision. The more balanced the decision, the more the potential for conflict. It is a bittersweet thing; they, out of necessity, must go together."

That doesn't sound very encouraging," suggested Cora.

"Now I understand," concluded Billy, "the need for a safe environment of respect and trust to overcome the inevitable conflict that accompanies every balanced decision."

"Let's get to the issue at hand, the secondary dam," championed Billy.

Peter suggested a design. The others adapted and adjusted Peter's design, taking advantage of the lessons learned from the main dam, operating within the respectful environment to which they had become accustomed.

Then the work began. Marc, teamed with Muddy and then Charlene, cut tree after tree precisely to fall with one end in the water, easy to cut and easy to maneuver to the dam site. Peter's team stripped the leaves and the bark for later food. Wise Brian led his group to trim the twigs to the right size and bring them to the dam as it was being formed. Muddy, the underwater expert, shifted her attention to firming the foundation and the mud packing between the twigs and tree trunks.

Billy showered the workers with words of encouragement and guidance. He led by example, diving into the water to check the dam's development and to secure a loose twig here and there.

By evening the secondary dam was done. Len admired the perfect curvature of the 100-foot structure and admitted it was as good a secondary dam as he had ever seen. Cora and Billy felt an overpowering sense of self-satisfaction.

Exhausted, the many beavers retired to the banks of the pond to nibble the bark, some twigs, and the profusion of fresh poplar, pine, and aspen leaves. Carol's team took up the first guard against any wolverines. For the rest of the evening they chatted about their families, their difficulties, and their pleasures.

"Any thoughts about a name for your dam?" asked Peter B.

"No," answered Cora, "have you some?"

"I do, as a matter of fact," stated the idea-ladened Peter B.

"Please share them with us," pleaded Billy.

"How about the 'Devon Dam'?"

"It sounds nice, but what does it mean?" asked Cora.

Peter paused, held his shaggy head back as if he were deep in thought, rubbed the shiny part, and then began to speak. "There is a sage animal many, many dams from here, in the land of the eagles, named Joel Eagle. His wisdom is acknowledged throughout eagle land. His nest is called the 'Devon Nest.' It is a huge and grandly designed nest. I think the name is appropriate here; he is a wonderful model to follow and I don't think he would mind. Some day, Billy and Cora, I hope to introduce you to Joel Eagle."

"I must admit 'Devon Dam' has a nice sound; I find it quite attractive."

"So do I," echoed Cora. "I think the name is terrific."

"Then it's agreed," confirmed Billy. He added: "I hope some day Joel Eagle will fly here so that we can meet him and show him what we have done and named in his honor."

"He owes me a visit; perhaps he will fly to meet us soon," concluded Peter B.

"On my trap line . . . it happened that I was running low in dog-feed . . . I decided to have a look . . . under the frozen surface [of a beaver lake]. I worked . . . for a whole hour to cut through four feet of ice . . . Imagine my surprise when I . . . [found] that there was no water underneath! . . . For a while I couldn't figure it out -- my final decision was that the dam at the other end of the lake [a mile and a half away] had burst. . . . I tied a rope to the sleigh and lowered myself down under. [T]hat lake was . . . empty and dry. Twenty feet deep, the water had drained away. . . . [I]n that empty lake there were icicles that looked like stalactites and stalagmites. . . . [A]fter the ice had formed [the trees from the bed of the lake] acted as columns. . . . The light in the cave was kind of greenish, any way [you looked], until you looked upward and then it was blue through the glassy dome . . ." **Tony Onraet (7)**

CHAPTER SIX
THE FOOD SANCTUARY

One by one they arose to prepare for the new day. Already, Mother Nature had started the metamorphosis in the pond. Small pond shrubs could be seen. Out of nowhere, frogs and tadpoles appeared—as well as snails and tiny minnows. A sanctuary had miraculously been created.

As they gathered to marvel at this spectacle that repeated itself for each dam, a sudden alarm sounded. Marc, Billy, and Cora ran to the front of the main dam. Below, Muddy was shouting and pointing her paw to the obvious collapse of the secondary dam. Water was pouring over the stream, forming a floodway instead of a brook. Fortunately the main dam held. Its sound structure was being tested and it was passing the test.

Muddy dove into the water, to the base of the secondary dam, to see if she could spot the problem. It irked her no end to think that something under her control was out of control, or that her *analysis* resulted in faulty construction techniques.

Then she spotted the breach—a huge gap in the base of the dam. She surfaced to report what she discovered and issued instructions for a few logs, more branches and twigs. She returned to the site, escorted by Marc, who now had become her friend. On close examination of the breach they could see a scattering of twigs. That was natural enough, but what could explain the logs wedged ten feet downstream from the bottom of the dam? Those logs had been pulled out by a group of beavers, for one lone beaver could not have done that.

A small conference was held.

"Obviously, this is the work of Albert," intoned Muddy. "I know— I know I'm not supposed to blame. But I'm just trying to explain what we have here."

"I would agree," offered Marc. "It is the work of a group of beavers; it wouldn't be one of us. Albert is a logical suspect."

"Our plan of action has to be twofold: repair the dam and prevent Albert or anyone else from sabotaging our work" suggested Billy.

"I'll set up a team to repair the dam," offered Muddy.

"I'll check out Albert and his gang," roared Marc.

"I'll join you, Marc," said Billy.

"So will I," offered Cora.

"May I accompany you?" asked Uncle Len.

"Of course," responded Marc. "You're always welcome."

The four beavers set off for the half-day's journey to the colony where Albert belonged. That colony was headed by a beaver called Danny the Trapper, for he was very wise to the ways of the beaver trap of humans.

This colony was noted for its innovative and *visionary* high-tech designs covering many beaver technologies. Called the Earthquake Dam, the colony was admired by all beavers in the region, and viewed as the only one that had an earthquake-proof dam. Danny received them warmly. Having heard about Cora, he was delighted to meet her and called out his *friendly* cohort, Roseanne, the beaver resources expert. Roseanne and Danny renewed their acquaintances with Uncle Len and Billy; and they met Marc for the first time.

After explaining the situation, Albert was called out by Roseanne and brought before the group. His reluctant attitude left no doubt in the foursome's mind as to who was carrying guilt.

"Albert, you twit, I know it was you and your buddies who destroyed our dam!" shouted Billy.

Danny looked on with disbelief; Albert was one of his most promising young engineers.

"Yes, I did it and I'd do it again if I could."

"Why, you little snot!" exclaimed Billy.

"You exiled me from the project," Albert said, pointing at Billy, "humiliating me in front of all those other beavers. I have a right to protect my interests."

"Protect your interests?" replied Billy in a high-pitched voice. "What interests? To topple trees and kill some beavers?"

Danny was dumbfounded. "Can this be true, Albert?"

"Beavers make mistakes; then one thing leads to another," defended Albert.

Uncle Len felt it was time for his intervention. "Danny, it's true and it's a difficult and common enough situation."

"Common situation?" questioned Billy and Marc in unison.

"Making mistakes is common enough, but where I'm leading is to the point that our most common instinct as beavers is to survive. This is true of all animals. It is common. Out of this instinct comes the need to defend our territory—not only our physical territory, but, in higher forms of animals, such as we beavers, to protect our *mental* territory. The moment someone accuses us of anything, puts us down, belittles us, we react defensively—we protect our mental territory."

"This is ridiculous," stated Marc. "Billy was right in expelling Albert. In fact, for all our safety he had to drum Albert off the project."

"Did I say anything about right or wrong?" asked Uncle Len. "Right or wrong, Albert's defensive mechanisms came into play, bypassing his logical senses through the brain's emotion center at a processing speed ten to one hundred times faster than the logic side. By having this fast defensive response, in a moment of crisis we have a chance to live to see another day. If we waited for our logic to tell us what to do, it might be too late. Billy, do you remember how quickly I bit that wolverine? And how alertly you rolled out of its grasp? Those were examples of our defensive instincts at play— no time to think things through. Well, these defensive responses take place during minor incursions into our mental territory, too. Our brain doesn't take time to figure out if it is minor or major, at least not till later when we occasionally regret our swift reactions."

"So we are supposed to be lovey-dovey while Albert destroys the world around us?" growled Marc.

"Get the notion of what you are *supposed* to do out of your minds for the moment. I'm trying to explain what happens during a fairly common event."

"Is Albert about to get off the hook?" demanded Cora this time.

"All right, let's get you guys some satisfaction. Albert's destruction of the dam was, no doubt, premeditated. At that point he behaved irresponsibly. What is the most important issue for you, Billy, with respect to Albert?"

"To get him to pay for his idiocy," demanded Billy.

"That's not what I heard you say at the dam site," reminded Uncle Len.

After taking a moment to pause and reflect, Billy continued: "I said that we had two priorities: to fix the damage to the dam and to prevent it from happening again."

"Billy, your search for 'justice' or revenge represents the emotion center of your brain in action. Before, when you were calm, you set your goal to prevent further damage. Let's take that more logical step."

41

Danny intervened. "It seems to me that Albert has some explaining to do. However, of this I can assure you: Albert will not set his paw in your territory for a long, long time, or until he is invited there by you. I'll make sure of that. Albert, do you understand me?"

Albert, looking at Roseanne, who tended to be more sympathetic than Danny, nodded a "yes" directly to Roseanne. Roseanne smiled weakly at the assembled group.

"This is an opportunity for you, Billy, Marc, and Cora, to be led by your logic and not your emotion center. Your goal has been achieved; Albert has been neutralized by Danny, who I sense is anxious to get to the bottom of Albert's misbehavior. We can now turn happily, with mission accomplished, to our own new Devon Dam."

"I'm trying hard to see the lesson you want us to learn, Uncle Len," asserted Cora, "but I'm having a lot of problems with it."

Marc spoke up. "It reminds me of my situation with Muddy last week. Nobody likes being accused, right or wrong. As soon as you blame, you head towards an escalating problem instead of a solution. If you love solutions, you will not go down that path." Marc paused.

"And what follows that?" asked Uncle Len.

"I have no idea," replied Marc, somewhat mystified.

"I'm at a loss," offered Cora.

Billy whispered an almost inaudible "Me, too."

It was Roseanne who filled the breach. "Uncle Len has shared his wisdom with our colony many times, and I think I know where this is going. What we all have to do is to be sensitive to escalating feelings brought about by the defensive path of the emotion center in others. We have to recognize that it strikes us at the same time, too, as we want to fight the counter-accusations. We also have an active emotion center. Instead, we have to focus on the other beaver and swallow our own egocentricity for a moment. We have to diffuse our emotional involvement. Otherwise we escalate the emotions and the defensiveness.

"So we let the accusation pass or the desire for revenge pass and focus on the issue at hand and calming down the other beaver. Uncle Len calls it 'diffusing emotions.' In this case you have to let your desire for revenge on Albert pass. This is probably an easier situation because you know that Danny Trapper will be taking care of things for you, one way or the other." Roseanne paused, indicating she had finished her explanation.

"Good response, Roseanne," said Uncle Len. "Let me add also, that diffusing is something you can learn to do. More importantly, it is something you *must* do if you want to get to the bottom of any issue. Emotions, the defensive response, will always work against a solution. You've got to neutralize or diffuse the emotion. The other beaver in the dialog with you won't, so *you* have to do it. If you want results, a solution to the issue at hand, you must deal with the emotional part of the dialogue."

There was a pause as the group pondered their newfound knowledge of dealing with beaver behavior. Uncle Len continued: "Learning to diffuse emotions doesn't mean you turn the other cheek. You must take action against all the threats out there. You unequivocally state your boundaries."

Billy, clearly agreeing with that part, jumped in. "Albert, make no mistake, our need to protect our environment will supercede any need we might feel to be nice to you."

Saying their farewells with a few slaps of their flat tails, the four beavers headed back to Devon Dam.

"Ralph Bice, one of Canada's most well-known trappers, tells of parking his truck before heading out to check his traps. On his return he found one flat tire. An investigation revealed that the puncture had been made by a large sharp beaver tooth . . ."
James Cameron (8)

"[A] government wildlife inspector at Sioux Lookout, Ontario, was live-trapping beaver in order to remove them to a more suitable area. He was using a wire trap with a trigger that closed the entrance to the cage once the beaver was inside. One cage . . . was closed every morning but there was never a beaver in it. . . . After several hours of waiting [and watching one night], he saw a large beaver appear; it pulled a stick from the dam and   . . . began poking at the trap . . . [until] it triggered the mechanism. . . . [He] observed this same procedure on several subsequent evenings. He never did catch this beaver."
Fred Bodsworth (9)

CHAPTER SEVEN
A LODGE TAKES SHAPE

When they arrived at Devon Dam, the four companions were delighted to find that not only had the secondary dam been returned to its fine shape, but Muddy had taken charge of construction of the lodge. Comprehending that Billy's plan was for a grand lodge, Muddy had ensured that a huge base was being formed of logs, sticks, and mud in the middle of the pond. Another change was that the pond was no longer a pond; it had expanded to form a huge lake. Marc scooped up a leafy, floating branch with his articulate paws, allowing his rudder-like tail to paddle him underwater to inspect the massive base now taking shape.

"You have been a *productive* beaver, Muddy," congratulated Marc. "I thought you were just good at *analyzing* details."

"I believe I'm good at both! In fact I think my desire for *analysis* drives my *productive* busyness," explained Muddy. But none of the newly returned beavers cared about an explanation—they were too delighted with the results before them.

However, Billy noted an ominous sign. Instead of the usual twenty beavers at work there were only about a dozen. "Where are Claude, Yvonne, Kathy and the others?" he asked Muddy.

"They quit. And good riddance, too! They were struggling with the tasks I gave them; they just didn't seem to learn."

Billy was now glad that he was back on the job. He decided that Muddy would continue to spearhead the construction of the lodge; but he would oversee to help reinforce the cooperation he knew was necessary, and could be applied.

As they added to the base, Billy noticed that Cherie was being asked to move heavy logs onto the next level of the foundation. She was grimacing at the task. "Muddy," he asked, "is not Cherie an *analyzer*, good at the details of applying twigs and mud?"

"Yes," responded Muddy, "but I like my beavers to learn all the tasks, even the gross ones in which *productive* busy beavers revel."

"From here it looks like Cherie is struggling with the logs, and she is not mixing with other beavers, which she, with her *friendly* disposition, is so good at."

"Yes, both observations are correct. But she's got to learn these other skills. I'm going to stay on top of her till she does."

"Muddy, my 'mba' training taught us that the number one reason beavers leave a job is due to dissatisfaction with the boss. They may give other candy-coated excuses, but the real reason is the relationship. The best guarantee of low turnover is a good working relationship between the boss and the workers," counseled Billy. "With half of your staff gone, perhaps you might review your methods."

"I can't stand whiners and snivelers. They've got to learn to take it; otherwise I don't want them here. This is serious business," Muddy informed Billy. "We've got to get rid of the non-producers."

Noting that Claudette, a *producer*-style beaver, was engaged in the *analyzer's* detail task of mud packing, and obviously not doing well at it, Cora was quick to add support to Billy's comments: "Some of those departed beavers produced very well under Billy's direction, didn't they?"

"Yeah, they had the right jobs, but this lodge construction demands something different," explained Muddy.

"There are times when we all have to do things we do not enjoy, but it should not be an *intentionally* chosen direction for a beaver," continued Cora.

"Yes," said Billy, taking up the challenge of getting these points across to Muddy. "Aren't you concerned about the defections?"

"Well, one part of me says, 'good riddance,' but deep down, I am concerned that I might not be doing things as well as I should," confessed Muddy. "What do you suggest, Billy?"

"I suggest that you do not fight the PAVF characteristics of beavers; PAVF represents their natural inclinations. It is permanently wired in. If you steer beavers towards their natural inclinations, they will thrill at the task instead of struggling with it. You want a group of beavers that get a charge out of their work, not dread it."

"Work is work; it is never easy," defended Muddy.

"Forget about other beavers for a moment, and think about yourself," suggested Billy. "You are not characterized as *friendly*. How would you like to be assigned a friendly job?"

"I wouldn't, but I wouldn't shrink away from it, either."

"Would it make you excited and eager every morning to rush to the job site to baby-sit a bunch of uncooperative beavers?"

"Well, not excited," conceded Muddy.

"How about slinging mud and twigs into the dam base or calculating the amount of materials required?" continued Billy.

"Well any beaver would be happy to do that!" said Muddy.

"No, they wouldn't," countered Billy. "You would; some others would. But many others would not—myself included.

"As an impatient *producer* you probably thrill at having something to do and get more thrills when you check it off your list. As an *analyzer*, I suspect you thrill when you can calculate the next dam materials list. But you do not thrill at *envisioning* or creating the next big project, and I know you do not thrill at being a *friendly* supervisor of masses of beavers; you'd prefer to do the task yourself and get it done 'right.'"

"I hate to concede; but generally what you just said is true," admitted Muddy.

"Here's the point, Muddy. If you select beavers for jobs in which they have their natural P, A, V, or F tendency, they will be eager and excited about doing the job; they will thrill to do it and then have a chance to excel at it, effortlessly. If you select them for a job at which they must struggle—as a natural consequence of who they are—they will just continue to struggle. They will learn slowly; they will not be happy; and with luck they may do okay at it. But they will never, ever excel at it.

"You can choose to make the workers *owners* of the job or *tenants* of the job. You can choose worker to have happiness, excitement, and thus excellence, at tasks or you can choose for them to have dullness, indifference, and thus a barely acceptable performance at it. Besides, guess which group needs more supervision?" questioned Billy in conclusion.

Muddy stopped to look at and think about her workers. She assessed the message from Billy and reformulated it in her own way: "Instead of focusing on beavers' weaknesses," she thought, "I must attempt to work with their individual strengths, accepting their 'weaknesses' as normal and essentially unchangeable. In that way I can benefit from their strengths and not get them, and me, frustrated over their weaknesses."

She thought: Cherie, Charlene and Branislav no doubt were *analytical* detailers; they would ensure that every stick was exactly in place, mud applied precisely into the cracks—and get great satisfaction from doing it. However, Claudette and Lee were busy *producers*, anxious to wrestle gigantic logs into place, the bigger the better. They would not be too fussy about the logs' exact fit. But the more massive the log, the happier beavers they seemed to be.

She began to plan her work accordingly. She called on Peter B. and Billy to *envision* ideas for the design of the living part of the lodge. They talked animatedly about options that Muddy, frankly, found quite uninteresting. But she noted that they were very excited about this design work.

She herself, as a detailed *analyzer*, along with Cherie and Charlene calculated the exact amount of twigs, branches, logs and mud to turn the twenty-foot-wide and twelve-foot-high design into reality. Branislav, or Branny, the other *analyzer*, was given the job of ensuring the materials arrived on time. Muddy could see the immense satisfaction on Branny's face as he controlled the arrival of the twigs down to the last stick.

True to form, Marc, Claudette, and Lee, as if driven by their *productive* busyness, heaved the big pieces into place with an energy Muddy found inspirational. Meanwhile, Cora provided nourishment of poplar leaves, sedges, ferns, and water plants for all the workers, giving them *friendly* encouragement for the challenges before them, and keeping them together as a cohesive force.

As time passed on the job, Muddy marveled at two things: first, all the beavers were happy in their assignments—no beaver was quitting or threatening to quit. Employed beaver satisfaction was being achieved.

Second, the above-water portion, the three-storey lodge, went up much faster than the foundation of the lodge, even though the lodge part was much more complicated to build than the foundation.

When the last twigs went onto the roof, leaving a hole at the peak for ventilation, all the beavers raised a congratulatory cheer for Muddy's successful and rapid completion of the lodge. Muddy herself admired Billy's youthful wisdom and silently thanked his precocious foresight for her success.

Uncle Len smiled contentedly, as Billy no longer consulted him, but had the confidence to address issues himself and to involve his team in their resolution.

"In the under-water world of the beaver pond the light from the cloudless autumn sun was tawny gold, now still as crystal, now quivering over the bottom in sudden dancing meshes of fine shadow as some faint puff of air wrinkled the surface. . . .

"The beavers, moving hither and thither through this glimmering golden underworld, swam with their powerful hind feet only, which drove them through the water like wedges. Their little forefeet, with flexible, almost hand-like paws, were carried tucked up snugly under their chins, while their huge broad, flat, hairless tails stuck straight out behind, ready to be used as a powerful screw in case of any sudden need."

Charles G. D. Roberts (10)

CHAPTER EIGHT
A HOME FOR CORA AND BILLY

Excitedly, all the beavers began to explore the grand lodge. The two entrances underwater were large enough for even the widest beaver to enter, but would exclude any predator. As they moved into the first level, they admired the chamber's spaciousness, dryness and apparent ease of removing the flooring material for cleaning. Its ample size meant that colony or family meetings could be readily accommodated.

Moving onto the second level, the beavers were proud of their accomplishment, for this, too, was ample, although not as large as the entry level. On one side were stored plenty of poplar leaves and white pine boughs, so Billy and Cora would have no food worries for some time. The storage would accommodate the long term—a full winter's supply of food. This eating chamber could house as large a family of kits as Cora and Billy might ever want to produce.

The thought of winter made Cora reflect on how, as a kit, she had followed her parents under the ice, finding air pockets to breathe quite readily. The temperature in the lodge was always above freezing, no matter how cold winter raged outside, protected by the lodge's six-inch-thick walls plus the added insulation of snow on the lodge itself.

Then, clambering onto the third level, they found that the last room was still of a magnitude that afforded considerable comfort. It had a sleeping area with boughs already in place, ready for Cora's and Billy's inaugural night in the lodge. They admired the high ceiling above them—its thickness and the interweaving of twigs and mud that made it strong and rainproof and would insulate Cora and Billy from the many cold blasts of winter that lay ahead of them. Muddy and her *detailers* had excelled on this roof.

Suddenly, the lodge began to shake above them. A few pieces of mud, not yet dried, fell upon them. The shaking did not pass. Marc scurried down the three levels, into the water and back up again to the surface of the pond as fast as his undulating tail would propel him to espy the source of the disturbance. It was a huge moose. The enormous animal had swum across the pond, attracted by, and now busily chewing on, the leaves protruding from the roof. It thought it had found an island of food and was taking advantage of what nature appeared to have provided!

Marc returned to the main chamber of the lodge, where the others were now gathered, and shared his discovery with them. They laughed at the novelty of it. Cora and Billy felt comforted, knowing that their roof would easily support the ravages of their enemy, the indigenous bear, who might try to collapse the lodge for a beaver dinner.

"Uncle Len," shouted Billy above the din, "do you have any final words of wisdom for all of us, before my friends leave for their own beaver lodges?"

Moving to the front of the group in the main assembly chamber, Uncle Len chose his words carefully.

"Cora and Billy, you have selected your management team well. You and they have engineered as fine a lodge and dam as I have ever seen—and I have seen many in my day. I may be stating the obvious, because I know it has been practiced by many of you these past few days; but it is important enough to merit reinforcement or to describe something you intuitively knew and to articulate it as a statement of wisdom for you.

"The only path to management success is the difficult path, the path of treating your workers as unique beavers, of caring for each one individually, one at a time. Each one is so different that he or she must be treated as unusual. Because they are unique, you must spend the time to find those differences or else you will never be able to take advantage of their individual talents. Often, beavers are unaware of their inherent talents, their thrills, and the tasks they are able to do effortlessly; so together, you and your individual workers have to take the time to discover them. You must focus on the strengths of your workers and not try to correct the weaknesses—that is attempting to push a round stick into a square hole.

"If you need so much time with your workers, you cannot have too many workers reporting to you. I believe the span of control should not exceed seven beavers. If you have more than seven, you cannot give them the attention you need to maximize their outputs. You will suffer in the long run.

"Contrary to what you may think, you need to spend *more* time with your good workers and *less* time with your poorer ones. There are many reasons for this, not the least of which is that you can learn from those who excel at their tasks.

"If you want more productivity you get it by assigning the tasks to those already proven to be able to produce, not by giving the tasks to unproven juniors. These are common mistakes I urge you to avoid. At the very least, think about these things as you move forward in your managing roles.

"There is a result that you will achieve that can be the measure of success with your workers. That occurs when you become in awe of what a specific worker can do. The more of your workers you admire, the more successful you will have been. That is because most beavers have some skill that is awesome. Your success comes when you discover it and can put it to use."

"Beaver are quite vocal and talk to each other frequently. As kits, they emit a high-pitched, almost mewing sound, which later develops into a lower-toned murmer. An angry beaver hisses and blows through its nostrils" **James Cameron (11)**

". . . a young beaver was lapping milk from a saucer while an Indian baby was pulling its fur. It was not until after several repetitions that I noticed that it was the cry of the beaver instead of the child." **Lewis H. Morgan (12)**

". . . Their voices were really the most remarkable thing about them, much resembling the cries of a human infant, without the volume but with a greater variety of expression, and at all hours of the day and night there was liable to be some kind of new sound issuing from the interior of the box. The best known and easist to recognize of these was the loud, long and very insistent call for lunch, which chorus broke out about every two hours."
Grey Owl (13)

CHAPTER NINE
ALONE AT LAST

After giving thanks to the many helpers and especially to Uncle Len, and having bade them farewell, Cora and Billy decided they would take a swim in the fresh water. They dove out of the lodge, into the pond, passed over the main dam, clambered over the secondary dam, spilled into the stream, and followed it to the river. In the larger body of water, they swam and cavorted, Cora wrapping her generous tail around Billy who thrilled at its touch. They giggled, laughed and guffawed, as much as any beaver couple could. They were having a good time. Sea, sand and cuddling—for what more could they ask? They were alone at last.

Returning up the stream, over the two dams, into the pond, and up to the great lodge, they became aware of some changes. As they moved into the main chamber Billy immediately was greeted by his father and his mother. Standing beside them Cora sensed, before she saw, her own parents. It was a joyful reunion for everyone. The older beavers expressed admiration for their keen youths and their magnificent accomplishments.

"You know, Father Beaver," began Cora, "we could not have done it without Uncle Len's guidance. His advice kept us in balance and on course. It helped us direct the other beavers who assisted us as we progressed. Billy was a magnificent leader."

"I'm not so sure about that," explained Billy modestly, "but Cora was always at my side when I needed her. Through the experience, we learned an awful lot together."

"Yes, we did," chorused Cora.

Over poplar leaves in the dining hall, Cora and Billy talked about the project with their elders. Billy's generosity led him to ensure a feast fit for the parents, so the event included the bark of willow, maple, birch, spruce, and balsam, and roots, grasses and fungi as the main course. For dessert, the offering was berries, water lilies, vegetables and fresh fruit.

The four adult beavers learned about the trials and tribulations, the difficulties and the disasters, that had brought Cora and Billy to this successful conclusion of the great Devon Dam.

"You know, Billy," suggested Dad, "perhaps you should summarize what you have learned. This will reinforce all the new information in your mind and make it easier for you to pass it on to your beaver kits when they become old enough to strike out on their own."

"I think that's a great idea," agreed Cora. "Besides, the kits may be closer to reality than you realize."

Billy gave Cora an astonished glance. Cora quickly asserted: "Let me begin with a few thoughts, if I may."

"Please do," suggested Dad.

Cora began without hesitation: "I would start with:

1. Don't be too proud to get some outside advice.
2. Stop to look at your problems that you *must* have accumulated. Resolve those first, otherwise your efforts to improve will be seriously impeded.
3. Learn the missing fundamentals of managing enterprises before you proceed, but only as you need those fundamentals. Solving the problems will tell you which fundamentals you need.
4. Until you have completed 2 and 3, problems and fundamentals, you cannot begin with new initiatives towards increased productivity, efficiency, and accountability; they will never work.

"Over to you, Billy."

"My first lessons," Billy voiced with authority, "are:

5. Don't lose sight of your intended results. As you progress, review those anticipated results often to be sure you are still on the right track.
6. Never rest on your laurels; otherwise you will develop a false sense of security and fail.
7. Don't be blind to obvious problems—especially when they come from those deemed to be successful.
8. If you're not having fun, something is wrong.
9. You never know when or where danger is lurking, except that it's always nearby."

"Especially if it's a wolverine!" added Cora. "That brings up my next points, which are:

10. Cooperation is a multiplier of effort. Two workers can become like four.
11. You must not trivialize the concerns of others.
12. Maintain a balance between short-term consideration and long-term considerations.
13. Out of adversity come opportunities."

Billy, sucking air past his incisors, indicated he was ready to add more thoughts. Cora paused to let him say: "It seems to me we have learned that:

14. By focusing on behavior problems, we eliminate technical problems.
15. Teachers always learn from students. So teaching is a two-way path.
16. Follow the 80% rule in new endeavors."

"Eighty birds in the hand are worth 100 in the bush?" queried Cora. "Almost, but not quite," chuckled Billy. He continued: "I would also suggest that:

17. Have faith that you will find the remaining 20% when you need it.
18. Do not apply the 80% rule to issues of accuracy or precision.
19. We learn by doing, not by watching."

"Yes . . . Uncle Len threw the leadership job at you right away. No, I'm wrong—at *us*," corrected Cora. She interjected: "That brings up other rules:

20. Only one individual can have the ultimate authority over a task.
21. To make balanced decisions you need to have all four of: *producers, analyzers, visionaries* and *friends*. Otherwise the decision will be skewed away from the missing ingredient.

22. We all have some of these, but none of us has all four of them. So it takes more than a group of one to make a balanced decision.
23. Conflict is an inevitable consequence of ensuring a balanced decision.
24. Good leaders allow workers to do the task their own way.

"Billy, I've gone on too long. Do you have any more to add?"

Billy turned to his silent audience: "Are we boring you to death? Mom? Dad?" There was a low-pitched laugh from the adults.

"No, Billy, you're not boring me," affirmed Dad.

"Nor me" offered Mom. "You have no idea how many of these I apply to our family and social situations. Please continue."

Billy, still full of enthusiasm, picked up the tempo from Cora. "It's easy from this dam building experience to see that:

25. If you don't instill respect and trust throughout the enterprise, you will not progress to the needed level of cooperation.
26. Respect and trust must begin at the top.
27. Because of the 'trust gap,' trust follows respect.
28. Take time to lay the proper foundation.
29. Resisting the temptation to profit early will reap large dividends later.
30. Placing blame on an individual will work against arriving at a solution.
31. You must involve apparently 'culpable' individuals when seeking the solution to a problem."

"I have more," added Cora. She noticed her adults shifting restlessly. "Billy, more leaves, bark, vegetables, or fruit for our dear parents. Okay, let's all take a break."

They moved their positions; then they nibbled on the fresh produce. Cora dove into the pond. Within minutes she returned with her paws full of water lilies, which she shared with them. They munched contentedly.

"Should I continue?" asked Cora.

"Well, I for one have had enough," said Billy's mother: "Enough food and enough education!"

"Me, too," offered Cora's father.

The other two adults expressed their desire to see what else had fallen out of the dam building experience.

"Please feel free to leave at this point," suggested Billy. "Go on to what else you would prefer to do."

The two adults shuffled out of the room, heading for the upper chambers, leaving two behind.

"For you who have decided to stay, we are delighted to complete this summary. Cora, it's your turn," indicated Billy.

Cora opened up with: "I have found from this major undertaking that:

32. If you want to resolve issues you have to diffuse emotions first, second, third and always.
33. To deal with transgressions, always define your boundaries.
34. The number one reason for a worker's departure from a job is a poor relationship with the boss.
35. Focus on those things that workers are naturally good at instead of focusing on their weaknesses.

"I know we're near the end. Billy, I think you should have the honor of wrapping up this summary."

Without missing a beat, Billy accepted Cora's baton. "Finally," he summarized, "we learned that:

36. To manage well, you have to view each worker as a separate and unique individual.
37. It takes time and effort to see to the needs of each of your workers; thus your span of control should not exceed seven workers.
38. If you want more output, get it from your best workers.
39. Spend more time with your best workers rather than your weaker ones.
40. You can measure your success by counting the number of workers you have brought to a level in which you have become in awe of their achievements."

The two adult beavers looked at the two youngsters in awe. It was only at that moment that they realized their own level of success as parents.

"To wrap up," continued Billy: "building a great dam is not easy, but it is quite doable by any beaver. Building it, while hard work, has to offer fun and a sense of self-worth. You must never lose sight of the purpose of building such a dam, namely to achieve the final results—for us, a constant food supply and a comfortable, secure home for us and our family now and for generations to come."

"Upon returning to his home in Fitzroy Harbour, Ontario, in the summer of 1975, Mr. W. G. Ward discovered that half of his raspberry bushes and a bushel of cucumbers had been taken from his garden by beaver from the Ottawa River." **James Cameron (14)**

"[We] dropped them aboard, two funny-looking [baby] furry creatures with little scaly tails and exaggerated hind feet, that weighed less than half a pound apiece, and that tramped sedately up and down the bottom of the canoe with that steady, persistent, purposeful walk that we were later to know so well. We looked at them in a kind of dumb-founded bewilderment. . . .

"[With time] they both acted much as if they owned the pond and environs, and certainly without them it would have been just a shallow, lifeless muddy sheet of water. Their presence there gave life to it, and imparted to the valley an indefinable air of being occupied that no other creature save man could give it. Many came to this hitherto deserted spot because of them. . . ." **Grey Owl (15)**

EPILOG

Well beavers, we have to lay a foundation for the great dam that we intend to build, or at least set the stage for its construction. We have to choose the right stream, the right place on the stream and the right foundation of mud, twigs, and sticks. Otherwise the waters will just flush the dam away. In the course of doing that, I find that there are ten rules to follow in order to create a successful enterprise that will endure over the long term.

The Ten Rules of Business

The ten rules for creating, running, and maintaining a great enterprise are:

a. Treat all stakeholders with respect and trust.

b. Preserve a visioning environment at all costs.

c. Align management before it starts building.

d. Rid yourself of excess baggage—you cannot ascend a peak carrying a heavy load on your back consisting of the hidden problems of the enterprise.

e. Take a break just before the final assault to the peak.

f. Learn who you are before you decide where you want to go.

g. Remember to plan—this provides a competitive edge and the structure to implement the plan.

h. Make sure feedback loops are in place—nothing gets done effectively without feedback loops for accountability.

i. Never rest on your laurels.

j. Keep the channels of communication open—everyone must know what is going on anywhere in the enterprise.

If you are committed to *consistent cooperation,* which is the prerequisite to achieving *excellence,* you can get there by observing these ten rules.

You have the immense challenge before you of achieving success for your enterprise—of having a group of people achieve amazing things; enjoy achieving amazing things; and enjoy each other while achieving amazing things. The opportunity for success includes the challenge of sustaining remarkable results over the long haul; that is, of not only achieving the goals before you, but also of: having a good scorecard (profits at the right time), having fun coupled with low staff turnover, generating sustainable growth, and finally, gaining peer recognition as acknowledgement from an outside world. When you arrive there, you will be at *Excellence.*

This challenge is both realizable and repeatable.

So, there are no more reasons for delays. Let's get going!

Good luck and have fun!

Bill Caswell
Ottawa, 2003

Appendix

The Best Dam Business Book in the World (Volume 1 of a set) is a summary of a more detailed book in progress entitled *The Climb to Excellence*, by Bill Caswell, and is the first of eleven more books to come of a how-to series for successful business operations. All twelve books are described individually below. The book, *The Climb to Excellence*, expands on the logic of choices for those who lead group endeavors. The larger the endeavor, the more important becomes the understanding and application of the logic of these choices.

That takes care of books #1 and #2; but why twelve books? The reason begins with the strong suggestion that you lay a solid foundation for your dam, and grow your enterprise from there.

Indubitably there are other approaches. But this is a documented self-help approach. As you pursue each step you will get measurable results that will reinforce your confidence that you are on the right path.

The Twelve Volumes

The twelve volumes (with apologies to beavers everywhere) are titled:

1. *The Best Dam Business Book in the World* (A fast-read summary of the set)

2. *The Climb to Excellence* (Building a great dam that will last)

3. *Saving the Enterprise* [from the inevitable] (Why great dams fail to survive)

4. *Setting the Agenda for Change* [in three days with reluctant staff] (Focusing on changing the dam instead of each other)

5. *Solving Impossible Problems* [every time] (Eager beavers have problems to resolve)

6. *The Pause before the Assault* [on the Peak of Greatness] (Preparations for the biggest dam job of all)

7. *Why Do Companies Exist?* (Why are we building the dam, anyway?)

8. *Planning, Strategy, and Structure* [that works] (Even beavers have to plan)

9. *Feeding or Starving the Organization* (Directing individual beavers towards outstanding efforts)

10. *Great Enterprises Never Rest* (Beavers do not have time to rest on their laurels)

11. *Getting Started in Business* (Pitfalls to avoid for those beavers wanting to start their own dam from scratch)

12. *The Balancing Act at Excellence* (The left-paw beaver must be informed to be in balance with the right-paw beaver)

Following All the Steps

It has been my experience that all ten of the procedural steps (Volumes 2 to 10 plus #12) above are needed. Believe me, I have tried to take shortcuts, but the absence of any one of the steps has left some of my in-a-hurry efforts with less than satisfactory results. I had to go back and pick up the missing pieces later. Ambitious to shorten my approach for smaller firms, to avoid burdening them with too much process—a noble aim, I think—I ultimately found the attempted shortcuts harmed more than they helped.

Below is an explanation of what each book entails and how it logically leads to the next step. Ten of the books, Volumes 2 to 10 plus #12, will each be an explanation of one of the ten rules above.

To take this book-like approach on your own, without external intervention, you should go through each of the ten volumes in order, excluding none of them—and including all the steps within them, unless otherwise advised in that book. The good news is that to execute each book will take months, so you have time to read and absorb each over a time span of, perhaps, two years. And if you're building for the long term, two years is but an instant. (Just look back two years ago and assess how quickly that has passed!)

1. *The Best Dam Business Book in the World (A fast-read version of the set)*

Often people need a kick-start to a change in their lives—more specifically, their business lives. Watching a colony of beavers agonize through the trials and tribulations of getting co-operation to build a great dam might whet your appetite for more information of how you can improve your own group endeavors.

2. *The Climb to Excellence*

The goal is to successfully build a great dam and to make sure it will last for future generations. The message contained in Volume 2, *The Climb to Excellence*, is that there is a workable answer to the question of how to run an enterprise well. Being successful is predictably possible, but it is hard work, and there is no shortcut. Success is having a group of people achieve amazing things, enjoy achieving amazing things, and enjoy each other while achieving amazing things.

Last, but not least, success includes sustaining success over the long haul. That can only happen if respect and trust become a way of life within the enterprise. For a corporation, this means not only achieving the goals before it, but also having a good scorecard (profits), having fun coupled with low staff turnover, generating sustainable growth, and, finally, gaining peer recognition as acknowledgement from an outside world. I call this *Excellence*. Getting there, I call *The Climb to Excellence*.

3. *Saving the Enterprise*

Studies confirm that there is a simple common denominator for companies that die ignominiously after having succeeded brilliantly.

Their insidiously unexpected collapses are not a mystery; they are totally predictable. Volume 3 explains what this simple predictive death knell is all about. It shows the complete evolution of the enterprise from conception to death and how all the stages in between are inevitable—or are they? More to the point, it shows predictive difficulties along the way. It identifies those difficulties that are natural to the beaver and that can be handled in their stride. It also identifies those issues that are unnatural to the beaver and that are therefore life threatening. The benefit from Volume 3 comes not only from thwarting your firm's early demise, but also defining how you can get to *Excellence*—and stay there as long as you want, despite the precariousness of the position of *Excellence* at the uppermost tip of the evolution pyramid.

With an understanding of evolution, you can predict your own future. More importantly, a CEO can take control of the company's future.

Taking that information in hand, where do you really begin to effect change? The next book starts the change process with a focus on you and your associates.

4. *Setting the Agenda for Change*

Like a group of meandering beavers, individuals in companies seem to be aligned in very different directions. The marketing department heads in one direction, sales in another. Engineering has certain processes quite unaligned with the purpose espoused by management. There must be a move from the silo mentality. Volume 4, on *alignment*, is the harbinger of the arrival of the head beaver to point the others in a common direction. Specifically, alignment of the teamwork processes is inculcated. A means to align all the identified problems before the organization follows. More important, there is an alignment of their priorities to the organization and hence their order of being resolved.

That done, the stragglers running off in all directions, followed by their own followers—who knows where—become aligned to where the company is headed next. At this point, the beavers gain an understanding of, and align themselves towards, a common change process for the whole pond brought about by the ideas of the construction of the dam. How can you hope to initiate the biggest change in your corporate history if the team is not aligned towards it? It is not uncommon, during alignment, to uncover 150 to 200 problems of an organization that need to be wrestled to the ground. It takes the next step to tackle this gruesome forest of problems, tree by tree.

5. Solving Impossible Problems

If 150 problems have been allowed to sit and fester for years, they will continue to sit and fester for more years unless something different happens within the beaver pond. At this stage, the process for problem solving is introduced, including a measure of the effectiveness of solving each problem. A process for automatically reviewing priorities takes place, making allowances for new problems that inevitably arise in any dynamic organization.

The demonstration of resolving issues that could not be solved before, or that were being ignored, becomes uplifting for everyone in the enterprise. Since problems affect people in the company at all levels, staff of all ranks must participate in their solutions. It is through this need for solutions that teamwork spanning the entire enterprise really starts to happen. The beaver group also develops the skill of becoming proactive regarding problems, solving them as soon as they float down the stream. These problems, the unwanted parasites under the skin of the beavers, are constantly impeding progress.

In a company, the problems preclude the company's being able to introduce real improvements. Organizational improvements are doomed to failure until the "parasites" that pervade the enterprise are permanently eradicated. Only then can the company commence *The Climb to Excellence.* Many roles have to be learned—Authority, Facilitator, Referee, Secretary-General—each critical to ensuring that every problem-solving meeting is time well invested. If you want to learn how to solve problems—every time—this is *the* step. If the irritating parasites are out of the way, once and for all, then we can get on with building the dam!

6. The Pause before the Assault

Undoubtedly, with the yoke of unwanted parasites off the beavers' furry hides, the beavers want to begin the ascent up the stream, unmolested and undistracted, to build the dam to be one that achieves a level of *Excellence.*

By this stage, all the participants will have invested great energy just getting to such a point. The past will be viewed as a series of hard-won battles, but worth every skirmish along the way. The beavers will look back at how they were before both the alignment and the resulting problem solving; they will quite admire their own progress—as measured by any standard. And well they should; 150 problems have bit the dust!

However, to begin the assault there has to be preparation. The road to *Excellence* is even more difficult than the major work already accomplished; the beavers want to be ready. A brief pause is needed to plan the mechanics of the assault to get the final parts of the dam in place. A quick look back is required to see if there are still any unwanted parasites left. There usually are; and so, an apparatus has to be set up to deal with them.

Transferring to the human domain of a seasoned group, a refresher on behavioral dynamics is not only needed, but with the experience to date, it will now be understood and appreciated. Here the team learns how to diffuse unstable emotions—discovering that most humans, as it happens, wrestle with unstable emotions—learning to take the bad stuff in their stride. This is indeed preparation for the fine-tuning of the enterprise to become unified in *Excellence.*

The ancients were aware of the need for a pause: six days of work and one of rest, or, a field that is fallow preserves the health of the long-term harvest. Even beavers understand the need for a pause before resuming construction of the dam.

7. *Why Do Companies Exist?*

The young beavers, assisting for the first time in a large project, want to know why the dam is being built here, at this time, and to serve whom. Many more mature beavers that have been doing it unquestioningly for years discover that they don't really know either, and are thankful for the inquisitiveness of the young.

The first tangible step of *The Climb to Excellence* for humans is the understanding of the reason the company exists and proceeding from there. Called the *mission,* it is comprised of three parts: purpose, vision, and values. A mission is a reflection of all the people in the company—not just a chosen few. To obtain everyone's contribution in a controlled and participatory fashion is critical to ensure company-wide buy-in.

The final product is not only a mission statement, but also an unequivocal statement of "who we all are and what we all stand for." It pervades the enterprise and becomes obvious everywhere via the company's Web page, sales literature, and, most importantly, people's day-to-day behavior. The mission is crafted with all stakeholders in mind—including clients. Staff members become aligned to the company purpose, thereby easily avoiding temptations to wander into outside domains. They all have a clear vision of where the company wants to be—the best widget maker in the world by 2010 to ensure a future perspective. And they know they can fall back on their core values in tight decision-making situations. To quote Peter Senge, "A company aligned with a common mission is truly an awesome force." (Ref. #16)

How can a company plan its future if it is not clear to everyone in the firm why the company exists? Or if the company members are not aligned to the same vision and values? How can it lay out a plan for its future?

8. *Planning, Strategy, and Structure*

No group can afford the luxury of not planning! Not even beavers. In this competitive swamp, the entire staff of enterprising beavers must be focused on the same dam objectives and not be scattered in their individual goals and implementation patterns. Otherwise the dam will never get completed.

For humans, planning is also a means to avoid the discretionary over-spending, wasting syndrome. The company must create a comprehensive annual plan that includes give-and-take exchanges to determine priorities, steps for planning in future years, and month-by-month budgeting, establishing its competitive advantage and setting stretch goals. It entails getting full company buy-in to the plan—that is, everyone's participation in the planning process before and after. And it creates action lists with follow-up processes. The strategy for the company over the next short term of one or two years must be in place by common design.

With a plan laid out—a strategy for moving forward—it now behooves the organization to create the structure that will implement that strategy.

While the structure is designed to achieve the strategy outlined for the enterprise, it must also assure that the common causes of typical organizational failure are overcome. The structure must allow visioning and innovation to be encouraged, and must ensure that delegation is moved down to the lowest levels of the enterprise; that administrative bureaucracy is kept in check; and that balances are in place such as that between efficiency and effectiveness, as well as the balance between short-term and long-term aspirations.

Out of proper planning will fall the first steps towards meaningful profits.

9. Feeding or Starving the Organization

Each beaver has to know what its job is, what the measure of good performance is, how it fits into the whole, and how it can be personally rewarded for outstanding effort in order to feel good about its contribution to the cause and its own life in general.

Just like the beavers, once the human-based organizational structure is conceived and put into place, it must be fed in order to be fully supportive of the enterprise and the plans for which it is designed. Otherwise you will be starving the organization. Which will it be?

First, every person must be held accountable, leading to the commitment of the staff and their intrinsic motivation, which is done through a rigorous system of accountability.

Accountability can be defined as a system wherein an employee accepts the job—its description, its authority, and the measure of its effectiveness—and is prepared to be personally rewarded according to the performance of that job. Accountability is a sequence of events based on closing a feedback loop so that the person knows when the job is going well, according to expectations agreed to and measured.

Second, a job description for each individual has to be developed. It is *not* a detailed list of all the tasks of a person, but a list of the effectiveness of the tasks. It's not what you do, it's the result or outcome you achieve for others that counts. A job description, called a "Job Measurement," needs to be brief in order to have a clearly quantified and understandable measure for each task—understood by the individual and by everyone around the individual.

The third resource feeding the structure is its information flow. To be effective in a job, the information must flow to the right people, in the right format, in the right amount, at the right time. Effectiveness in a job expands to effectiveness of a department and finally to the effectiveness of the entire enterprise. Information flow tells if the enterprise is on the right track; the recipient continually monitors and adjusts against agreed-upon measures of success.

Fourth, beginning at the smallest level of work, proper behavior must be reinforced, and improper behavior discouraged. All humans and animals learn and improve their directions that way. Task-by-task, job-by-job, department-by-department, rewards and praise if properly applied are what make improvement possible.

Finally, this bottom-up approach takes the job measurements, accountability measures, information flow, and reward system concepts for individuals, and transfers them to business units throughout the enterprise. Categories of profitable, break-even, and support units are assigned according to the strategic purpose of the units. Thus, an integrated company-wide accountability pattern is established with financial responsibility matching authority so that results clearly tie to persons responsible for them, at all levels. Also, reward must be considered across the enterprise, so that myths are tackled; rewarding one group does not become a disincentive for the others; and rewarding for the short term does not jeopardize the long term.

10. *Great Enterprises Never Rest*

Beavers cannot rest on their laurels. Complacency will allow water to overrun the top of the dam, carrying twigs downstream, slowly eroding the magnificent structure.

Nor can a company at *Excellence* rest on its laurels. To ensure the company will enjoy staying at *Excellence* and not be allowed to silently slide into other, inferior, stages, managers must focus on defeating the twin demons of complacency and arrogance that usually accompany success. A program focused on maintaining *Excellence* has to be installed for the perpetuity of an enterprise that is already doing very well—enjoying its great position.

Power corrupts. Simply put, humans are prepared to be overly self-congratulatory, which leads to the downfall of great enterprises and great nations that we all can predict so easily. What are the signs of downfall? To prevent the company following that unnecessary trend, it requires a program of vigilance. The organization must maintain an open mind and an open door to new ideas. Questions have to be encouraged from the lowest levels. And its top people must listen. They have to continuously be humble. The world is changing, so the successful enterprise will take new steps to do new things well, too. Its focus will be outside, not inside. Past records mean almost nothing; it is the future that means so much. As in the other programs above, simple processes in these stages compensate for simple human weaknesses.

11. *Getting Started in Business* (Pitfalls to avoid for those beavers wanting to start their own dam from scratch)

"Aha, but I don't have a business yet; I want to create one," you say. For anyone in that position, Volume 11, *Getting Started in Business,* provides insights collected from the school of hard knocks of how to begin—but balanced with the wisdom of the earlier volumes.

12. *The Balancing Act at Excellence*

No beaver is an island. To keep the lodge in place, the main dam, the secondary dam, the planned spillage, the food supply, the pond, and its community, the group of beavers has to have access to the necessary information. How high is the water level, what is the flow rate, etc.? The left-paw beaver must know what the beaver on its right paw is doing and how each role fits into the big picture.

ABOUT THE AUTHOR

Bill Caswell, B. Eng., P. Eng., founder of Caswell Corporate Coaching Company (CCCC), was previously a co-founder and CEO of an e-learning company and three other high-technology enterprises. Bill was the president of the SPS division of a $100 million conglomerate, itself part of a $1 billion company. SPS was an information technology company, with offices in Ottawa, Toronto, Halifax, Seattle, and Guadalajara, Mexico. Bill sold SPS in 1996.

Earlier, as a design engineer, Bill was responsible for a number of inventions in the radar field, process instrumentation domain, and spent his early career with the Guided Missiles Range Division of Pan American World Airways, launching 200 scientific rockets per year into the upper atmosphere.

Besides English, Bill speaks Spanish. He is the author of many technical papers and one book: *Notes to My Children*. Bill, a dedicated family man, is also an avid downhill skier, an opera lover and a construction builder, adding to his family's five-bedroom ski chalet every year.

NOTES

1. Cameron, James M., *The Canadian Beaver Book* (Burnstown, Ontario: General Store Publishing House Inc., 1991), 78.

2. Ernie Michelburgh, *The Toronto Star* (October 23, 1983), quoted in James Cameron, *The Canadian Beaver Book* (Burnstown, Ontario: General Store Publishing House Inc., 1991), 123.

3. Cameron, James M., *The Canadian Beaver Book,* 145.

4. Bodsworth, Fred, "Castor the Canuck Makes a Comeback," *Maclean's* (July 15, 1950), quoted in James Cameron, *The Canadian Beaver Book,* 149–50.

5. Hearne, Samuel J., *A Journey from Prince of Wales' Fort in Hudson Bay to the Northern Ocean, 1769–1772,* Richard Glover, ed. (Toronto: Macmillan of Canada, 1958): 157, quoted in James Cameron, *The Canadian Beaver Book,* 121.

6. Cook, Helen and Lloyd, *Scrapper the Beaver* (Barrie, Ont.: self-published, circa 1985), quoted in James Cameron, *The Canadian Beaver Book,* 124.

7. Onraet, Tony, *Sixty Below* (Toronto: Jonathan Cape, 1944), quoted in James Cameron, *The Canadian Beaver Book,* 178.

8. Cameron, James M., *The Canadian Beaver Book,* 151.

9. Bodsworth, Fred, "Castor the Canuck Makes a Comeback," *Maclean's* (July 15, 1950), quoted in James Cameron, *The Canadian Beaver Book,* 148.

10. Roberts, Charles G.D., *The House in the Water* (Boston: The Page Company, 1916): 36–8, 50, 55–6, quoted in James Cameron, *The Canadian Beaver Book,* 175.

11. Cameron, James M., *The Canadian Beaver Book*, 82.

12. Morgan, Lewis H., *The American Beaver: A Classic of Natural History and Ecology* (New York: Dover Publications, 1986): 222, quoted in James Cameron, *The Canadian Beaver Book*, 122.

13. Grey Owl, *Pilgrims of the Wild* (London: Penguin Books, 1983): 37, 39, 182–83, quoted in James Cameron, *The Canadian Beaver Book*, 177.

14. Cameron, James M., *The Canadian Beaver Book*, 151.

15. Grey Owl, *Pilgrims of the Wild* (London: Penguin Books, 1983): 37, 39, 182–83, quoted in James Cameron, *The Canadian Beaver Book*, 177.

16. Senge, Peter, *The Fifth Discipline* (New York: Doubleday/Currency, 1990).

INDEX

80% rule, 20,21,63
Accomplishments, 7,10.33,55,61
Accountability; 13,62
Accuracy, 20,63
Achievement, 10
Adversity, 14,63
Advice, Advisors, 9,62
Analyzer, 22
Appearances, 13
Authority, 21,29,63
Awe, 7,57,65,66
Balance,
  maintaining, 13,20,23,29,61,63
Behavior, 15
Blaming, 34,39,42,64
Blindness, 10,62
Boss, 48,65
Boundaries, 43,65
Bureaucracy, 10
(Business) Process
  Re-engineering, 10
Busy, 7,34,50
Chaos, 23,27
Champion (business), 12
Characteristics, 22
Communicating, not, 7
Concerns, 12,27
Conflict, 10,23,35,64
Cooperation, 11,14,27,28,63
Culpable individuals, 34,64
Customer satisfaction, 8
Danger, 62
Decisions, 23,29
Decisions,
  balanced, 23,30,35,63,64
Defensive, 41

Delays, 21
Delegate, 21
Difficulties, 56
Diffusing emotions, 42,65
Disaster, 21
Discipline, 4
Effective, 9
Efficiency, 62
Emotions, 42,65
Epilog, 67
Excel, 49
Expert, 10
Fail, 5,15,62
Fine-tuning, 13
Focusing, 42
Foundation, 8,64
Friend, 22
Fun, 7,10,62
Fundamentals, 8,9,14,62
Goals, 10,15
Groundwork, 29
Hard work, 7
Improvement, 33,62
Initiatives, new, 10,15,62
Indifference, 7,49
Innovation, 10
Instincts, 41
Job satisfaction, 48
Laurels, resting on, 10,62
Leaders, 21,29,61,63,64
Leaving a job, 48
Learning, 12,14,15,35,61,62,63
Logic, 41,42
Long-term, 4,13,63
Luck, 4
Managing, 14,15,62

Mba, 3,8,48
Meetings, 14
Mess, 10
Mission, 7
Mistakes, 40,57
Mood, 10
Multiplying results, 14,63
Myths, 9
Objectives, 8,13
Obstacles, 15
Opportunities, 14,27,63
Output, 65
Partnership, 4
PAVF, 24
Peer respect, 9
Personalities, 22,23,30
Priority, 12,41
Problems, 8,12,13,15,62
Process, 4,14
Producer, 22
Productivity, 57,62
Proficiency, 13
Profits, 7,8,30,64
Progressed, 61
Proud, 62
Proven process, 4
Ready, 10
Reasons, 48
Relationship with boss, 48,65
Resolving issues, 8,50,62,65
Respect, 9,28,64
Results, 7,13,62
Return (on investment), 13
Rewards, 13
Right, getting this business, 3
Sales, attracting, 8
Satisfy, 8,50
Shortcuts, 4

Short term, 13,14,63
Signs of problems, 9
Skeptical, 8,10,12,15
Smart work, 4
Solving, 34,42
Span of control, 56,65
Stakeholders, 30
Stifling, 10
Strengths of workers, 49,56
Struggling, 47,48
Success, 10,14,50,56,57,65
Suffering, 10
Survival, 11,40
Teamwork, 50
Technology, 40,63
Time constraints, 20
Transgressions, 40,43,65
Trivialize, 12,63
Trust, 28,64
Unquestioning, 9
Visionary, 22
Waves, making, 9
Weaknesses of workers, 49,56,65
Workers, 49,65

To order more copies of

THE BEST
DAM
BUSINESS BOOK
IN THE WORLD

Contact:

GENERAL STORE PUBLISHING HOUSE
499 O'Brien Road, Box 415
Renfrew, Ontario Canada K7V 4A6
Telephone: 1-800-465-6072
Fax: (613) 432-7184
www.gsph.com

VISA and MASTERCARD accepted